THE KIND BEE
JUST BEE CAUSE

Written By Justin & Jaime Clarke

Illustrated by Debra Goley with
Assistance by Hayley Clarke

THE **Honey** FOUNDATION
Just BeeCause

1982 2011

S C

Scott Thomas Clarke
Forever Loved – Never Forgotten

Our Inspiration

The Honey Foundation is a Goodyear, Arizona based non-profit, with a mission of making the world a better place through random acts of kindness. The Honey Foundation was founded by Justin and Jaime Clarke in 2012 in memory of Justin's identical twin brother, Scott.

Every Mother's Day, Scott would give the cashier at a local Starbucks cash and roses, asking the clerk to please use the cash to pay for every mother's coffee - including a rose - until his money ran out. He didn't ask for recognition or repayment of any type. His only wish was that the receivers would soon pay it forward, too.

On Mother's Day 2011, Scott's Mom, Mary Ann, went to Starbucks to buy a coffee. After ordering, she found that someone else had already paid for her coffee, and then received a rose. While waiting on her drink, she asked, "Who on Earth could have done such a kind deed?" The answer: her own son, Scott Thomas Clarke.

Sadly, June 3, 2011, Scott passed away at age 29. After Scott's memorial, his stories of kindness inspired more, as a group of his friends collected money to 'Pay It Forward' on Father's day, in Scott's honor, at the same Starbucks that Scott did a month earlier.

Scott's Pay it Forward came full circle. Kindness spreads fast.

The Honey Foundation was created on September 11, 2012 in legacy of Scott, and the importance of Kindness. #BeeKind #JustBeeCause

THIS BOOK BEE-LONGS TO:

_____

In the quiet desert morning, the sky turns light from dark, and a hive of honeybees wake up, at a place they call Scott Park.

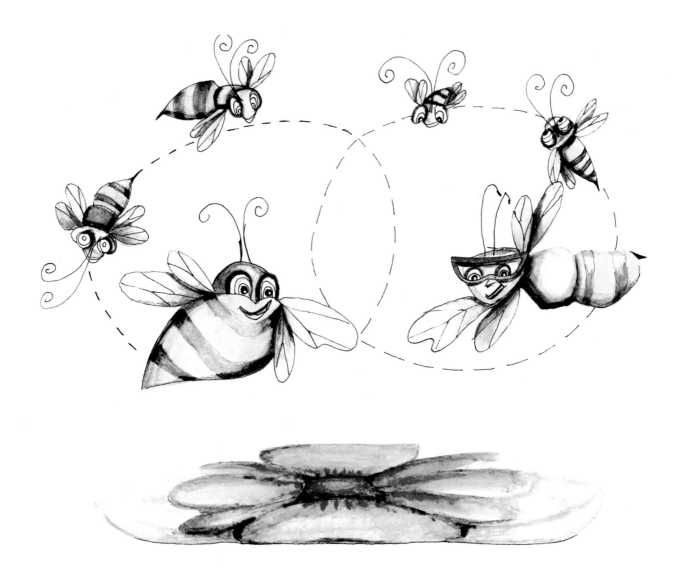

Benny and his honeybee mates, get ready for the day, soaring off to Flight School, with their friends to learn and play.

Since Benny was a larvae, he was a different kind of bee, he had all of the same markings, but no stinger there to see...

The other bees, didn't treat him the same, they hardly ever played with Benny, and even called him names!

"Benny looks so different," the other bees rued,
"Don't get caught playing with him, or you'll lose your stinger, too!"

A buzz for class hums loud above, and the honeybees join together
to sing, but as they pass poor Benny, they give him each a sting.

Honeybees we are, flying from flower to flower,
we might be small and winsome,
but our **Stingers** give us all our power."

Benny peeked around his home, and much to his surprise, the trees in Scott Park weren't as vibrant, and all the plants were starting to die.

At honey-time, Benny flew to see the queen, "Scott Park is the worst that I've ever seen," Benny buzzed, "And all the bees want to do is sting and sting! The Queen said in response, "If you want the other bees to change, set the example of kindness, and ask for nothing in exchange."

Later that day, Benny saw a friend flying alone, so he asked if he could be her wingman, until the time to go back home. "Rose, you're the best friend I could find, would you mind helping me tomorrow, do something kind?"

Together, Benny and Rose made a plan...
they would perform Acts of Kindness, for whoever they can.

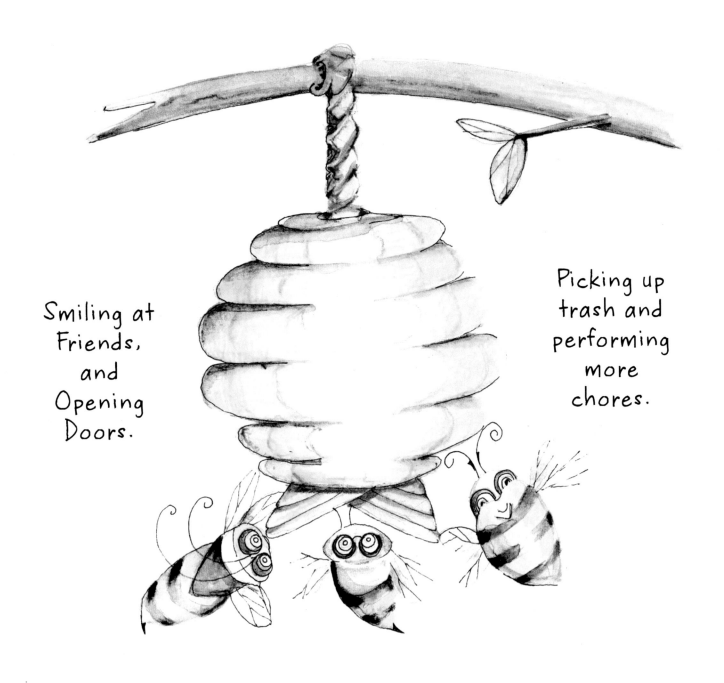

Smiling at
Friends,
and
Opening
Doors.

Picking up
trash and
performing
more
chores.

Bandit and the other honeybees all joined in if they could—
"Hey, doing kind things all day actually feels really good,"
Bandit buzzed.

Soon enough, their kindness did spread.
Rather than stinging all day,
the bees were doing nice things instead!

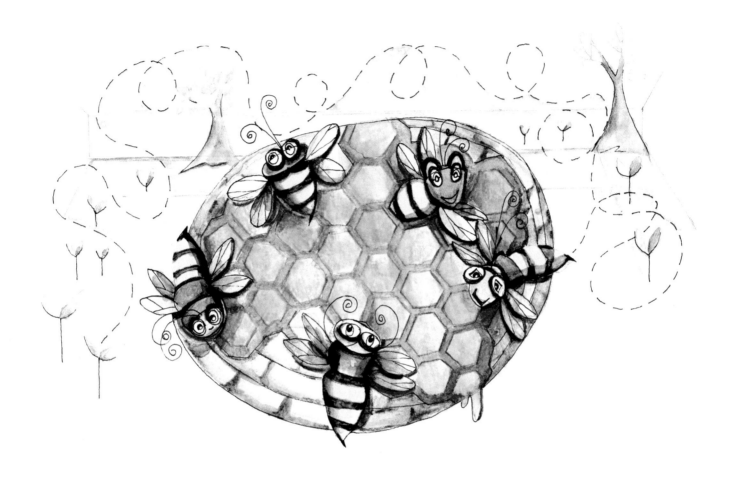

By the end of the day, working together for hours, the bees realized it wasn't their stingers that gave them their powers.

 "Honeybees we are, flying from flower to flower,
we might be small and winsome,
but our **Kindness** gives us all our power."

Bandit and the other bees felt so much better, "Maybe our stingers aren't always the answer," "Lets take off our stingers," Bandit said, "And we'll keep pollinating kindness instead."

Benny and Rose were so happy to see, that kindness actually set them all free. Instead of stinging, as it was, all the other bees were being kind, *just-bee-cause*.

In a matter of time, Scott Park returned to it's beauty,
and all the bees learned that being kind was their duty.

The bees lived happy in their hive,
knowing that pollinating kindness keeps them alive.

The world can change, from one kind bee, the rest will happen,
you will see. Just bee kind to whoever is in range,
soon enough – the world will change.

Our vision is a world dedicated to kindness.

#BeeKind #JustBeeCause

The Honey Foundations is a 501c3 nonprofit organization that believes the world receives hope, through kindness.

In 2012, THF created Kindness Education Programs (KEP) for K-12 schools, clubs, and organizations alike. KEP was developed to teach others about the profound impacts of performing acts of kindness, including basic life-skill teachings about positive self esteem, confidence, effective communication, positive thinking, leadership, philanthropy, and the importance of a community. These social learning programs are designed to teach students that Kindness leads to happiness and success in life.

Honeybees are our inspiration bee-cause they pollinate the world with their kindness, helping fertilize plants, flowers, trees, and making honey. Without honeybees, our world would be a dark place: no flowers, no food, no love, no honey, and no kindness.

Our vision is to live in a world dedicated to kindness. One simple act of kindness can change the world.

KEP results indicate that kindness learning increases the sense of safety and security in our communities, as well as improve active participation, confidence, leadership and positive relationships between communities.

Published by The Honey Foundation
HoneyFoundation.org

Design and Artwork © 2018 Debra Goley Art
Assistance by Hayley Clarke
DebraGoleyArt.com

ISBN: 9781707589807

SUMMARY: The Kind Bee is a story about a young honeybee, Benny, who learns the importance of benevolence, and how simple acts of kindness can eventually change the world.

The Honey Foundation
BeeKindToday.org
Jaime@HoneyFoundation.org

Proceeds from "The Kind Bee Just Bee Cause" Book will benefit The Honey Foundation and Kindness Education Programs for K-12 schools.

PRACTICE KINDNESS

Bee Kind to others,
Bee the change in the world,
Bee-lieve in yourself,
Bee the difference maker,
Just BeeCause!

 Keep track of your good deeds!

_____ _____
Date   Random act of kindness

_____ _____
Date   Random act of kindness

_____ _____
Date   Random act of kindness

_____ _____
Date   Random act of kindness

_____ _____
Date   Random act of kindness

Get ideas & inspiration at beekindtoday.org

Made in the USA
Monee, IL
29 January 2023

26512548R00017